BARYONYX

by Janet Riehecky
illustrated by Jim Conaway

THE
CHILD'S
WORLD

MANKATO, MN

Grateful appreciation is expressed to
Bret S. Beall, Research Consultant,
Field Museum of Natural History, Chicago,
Illinois, who reviewed this book to
insure its accuracy.

Library of Congress Cataloging in Publication Data

Riehecky, Janet, 1953-
    Baryonyx / by Janet Riehecky ; illustrated by Jim Conaway.
        p. cm. — (Dinosaur books)
    Summary: Presents facts and speculations about the physical
characteristics and behavior of this fish-eating dinosaur.
    ISBN 0-89565-622-1 (lib. bdg.)
    1. Baryonyx—Juvenile literature.   [1. Baryonyx.   2. Dinosaurs.]
I. Conaway, James, 1944-   ill.   II. Title.   III. Series: Riehecky,
Janet, 1953-   Dinosaur books.
QE862.S3R5318   1990
567.9'7—dc20
                                                        90-2472
                                                          CIP
                                                           AC

1 2 3 4 5 6 7 8 9 10 11 12 R 98 97 96 95 94 93 92 91

BARYONYX

When the dinosaurs lived, they often had just one thing on their minds— FOOD!

Whether a dinosaur was a plant eater or
a meat eater, getting food was a full-time
job.

Some big dinosaurs lumbered through
the forest, stripping the leaves from the
trees.

Some little dinosaurs stole into the nesting grounds. They darted in quickly and grabbed some eggs.

There were dinosaurs that enjoyed a
bite on the run . . .

and others that settled for anything they could find.

Scientists have even found evidence that at least one type of dinosaur went fishing for its food. That dinosaur was the Baryonyx (BAR-ee-ON-ix).

Scientists know the Baryonyx was a meat eater because it had the sharp curved teeth needed to cut through meat. But in many ways, it was different from other meat-eating dinosaurs.

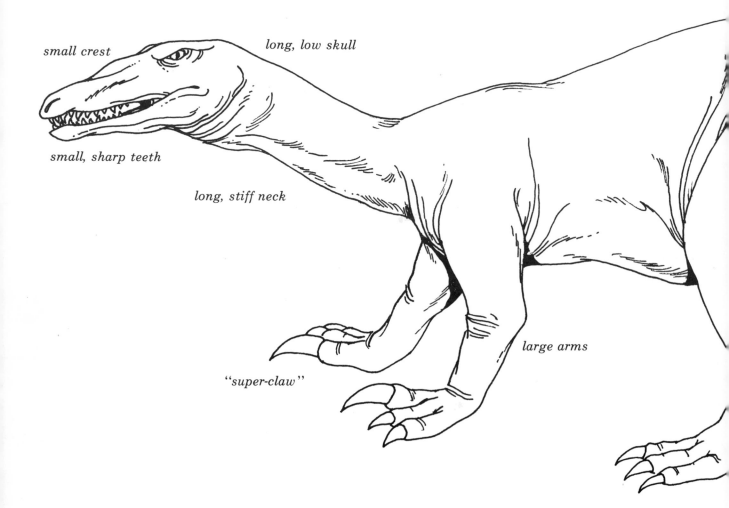

small crest

long, low skull

small, sharp teeth

long, stiff neck

"super-claw"

large arms

Most meat-eating dinosaurs had strong jaws, heavy skulls, and enormous teeth so they could slice through tough skin and bone. But the Baryonyx's jaws were not all that strong, and its head was long and flat, like a crocodile's. Its teeth were much

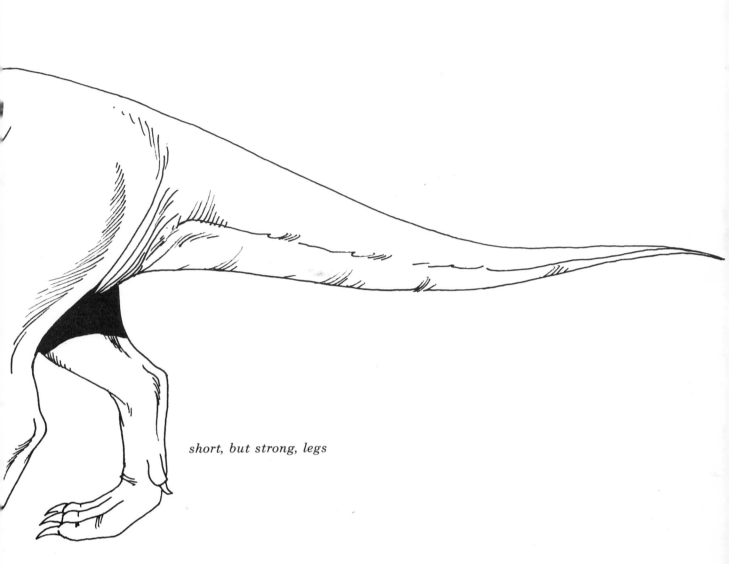

short, but strong, legs

smaller than most meat eaters'—and it had almost twice as many of them as other meat eaters had. The Baryonyx was not made for attacking other dinosaurs. It was made for catching fish.

A lot of animals like the taste of fish, but it takes a very special kind of animal to catch them. Fish dart about very quickly in the water. To catch them, an animal has to be even quicker. Fish are also very slippery. Holding onto them takes special claws or teeth.

So, how could the Baryonyx catch fish? Scientists have suggested several ways.

The Baryonyx might have stood by the edge of a shallow lake, waiting as patiently as a heron. When an unsuspecting fish swam by, the Baryonyx may have snapped it up. Its long mouth and many sharp teeth could have grabbed a quick-moving fish and held onto it no matter how much it wiggled.

Or the Baryonyx might have played crocodile. Some scientists picture it floating in the water, watching carefully. If a fish swam by, it was scooped up in the long mouth of the Baryonyx.

Another way the Baryonyx might have
fished was with its front feet. The Baryonyx could use its front feet as hands. It
had long, slender fingers which may have
been used to grab fish.

If the Baryonyx didn't feel like grabbing, it might have gone "spear fishing" instead. The name Baryonyx means "heavy claw." It got this name because it had a huge claw, the biggest dinosaur claw that has ever been found—twelve inches long! That's almost as long as your arm is up to the elbow.

Scientists picture the Baryonyx as having one of these "super-claws" on each front foot. So, when a fish swam past, the Baryonyx could stab quickly into the water and catch itself a fish.

Scientists know the Baryonyx ate fish because they found fish scales in one's stomach. But that wasn't all they found there. There were also a few bones of a large plant-eating dinosaur. How did the Baryonyx hunt large plant eaters when it wasn't a very strong dinosaur? Well, many scientists think it let a powerful meat eater like Megalosaurus do all the work.

A big meat eater like Megalosaurus could easily kill most plant-eating dinosaurs. After it did, it probably wouldn't eat the whole thing. The Baryonyx could come by afterwards and eat the leftovers.

So, the life of the Baryonyx was like a vacation—lots of fishing and free lunches!

The world the Baryonyx lived in was a beautiful world, bursting with many different types of plants and animals. There were huge, lush forests, and the ground was carpeted with thick ferns. For part of the year, the air was warm and wet. The rest of the year, it was warm and dry. There were many rivers and lakes full of fish. The Baryonyx lived in the lowlands, near the water, where it could find food easily.

Scientists can't say much else about how the Baryonyx lived in its world. They don't know whether the Baryonyx stayed by itself much of the time or lived with others in a herd or pack. They don't know whether the Baryonyx laid eggs or bore its young alive. And they don't know if it took care of its babies or left them on their own.

Scientists do think that the Baryonyx didn't worry much about protecting itself from bigger meat eaters. For one thing, it was a fairly big dinosaur, growing from thirty to thirty-three feet long and standing almost twice as tall as a person. For another, even though it wasn't a very strong dinosaur, its "super-claw" made a great weapon. Only a very big and very hungry meat eater would have bothered the Baryonyx.

Scientists have been trying to find out more about the Baryonyx since it was discovered in 1983. It is an interesting dinosaur because it is so different from other meat eaters. It and other recently discovered dinosaurs have helped to change some of the ideas scientists once had.

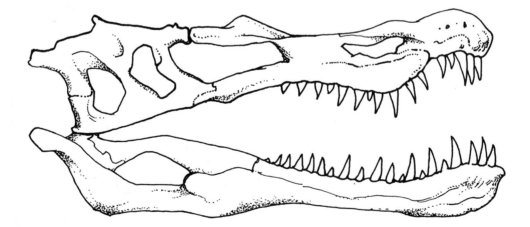

Scientists used to compare dinosaurs to living reptiles, such as lizards. Lizards are cold-blooded. This means they use the sun to warm their bodies. After they soak up enough heat, some can move around actively for a short time. But as soon as they cool down, they slow down.

Because dinosaurs were reptiles, scientists pictured them the same way. Scientists thought dinosaurs could soak up enough heat to move quickly for a short time, but that most of the time they were slow-moving creatures.

New dinosaur discoveries have made some scientists change their minds. Many dinosaurs had long, strong legs that seemed made for running fast and far. The Baryonyx did not have long legs, but it must have been quick-moving and active to catch fish. Many scientists now think it might be better to compare dinosaurs to warm-blooded animals, especially birds. They have even found nesting grounds which show that some dinosaurs nested and cared for their babies much as birds do today.

Studying dinosaurs is more interesting now than ever before. And new discoveries are adding to our picture of how the dinosaurs lived.

Dinosaur Fun

Were dinosaurs cold-blooded or warm-blooded? What's the difference? As you have read, it makes a big difference to scientists. If dinosaurs were cold-blooded, that means their body temperature went up and down with the temperature of their surroundings. But if they were warm-blooded, that means their body temperature stayed about the same on a hot day as on a cold day.

Birds and mammals are warm-blooded. Reptiles, amphibeans, and almost all fish are cold-blooded.

Make a poster to help you remember which animals are warm- and which are cold-blooded. Look through magazines and newspapers for pictures of animals from each of the 5 groups of animals named above. Draw a line down the middle of a poster board. At the top of one side, write "Cold-blooded" in blue. At the top of the other side, write "Warm-blooded" in red. Glue or tape the picture of each animal to the side where it belongs.